WHEN GOD SMILES

Erick Wright

Dedication

To my sons Dorian, Evan, Logan, Landen, William, Daniel, and Aiden.

The message in this book is dedicated to you my sons and every prince alike that will one day become king. The message is to know thy self. Understand who you are, your history, and your connection to this planet. It is our responsibility to understand, preserve, and protect. So, we gladly share our experience with all who wish to go far together. I love you all!

Remember:
God is love!
God is peace!
God is you!
God is me!

God smiles,
sun shines.

When sun shines,
trees grow.

Trees grow,
when sun shines.

The sun shines, my skin glows.
God smiles at my skin's glow.

When sun shines,
my hair coils.

God smiles at
my coiled hair.

Sun shines, the lions roar.
God smiles when lions roar!

We smell flowers in the sunshine.
God smiles as we play and smell flowers.

When God smiles

Trees grow!

Skin glows.

Hair coils.

Flowers smell.

LIONS ROAR!!!!

The End.

About Author

Erick Nathan Wright was born in Demopolis, Alabama and has accomplished an undergraduate degree from Troy University's Risk Management and Insurance program as well as a Master's in Public Administration. Erick has been a staple in the community especially to young men from broken families as a mentor and friend. From running for Congress in 2014 and receiving over 40,000 votes, being a part of the movement that removed the confederate flag to walking 15 hours from Montgomery to Selma Erick always strives for hard work and progression.

Erick is the owner and operator of Nathan's Insurance Agency and to many is known as the voice of the people that always "Just Think Wright." As the father of seven boys he realized that his children did not have valid access to books that provide reading phonics and cultural relevance. Erick is a strong believer in science, history and the imagination. He intends to introduce works composed of these characteristics to schools and libraries across the globe.

"If our children become more interested in reading today,
they can avoid the prisons of tomorrow."
~Erick Wright